Look In the

By Pamela Chanko

ISBN: 978-1-338-88850-8

Editor: Liza Charlesworth
Art Director: Tannaz Fassihi; Designer: Tanya Chernyak
Photos ©: Vicki Jauron, Babylon and Beyond Photography/Getty Images.
All other photos © Shutterstock.com.

SCHOLASTIC INC.

There is a cloud.

There is a plane.

There is a bird.

There is a helicopter.

There is a balloon.

There is a rainbow.

There is a kite!